Tony BLAIR

Biography

Tony BLAIR

Thomas M. Collins

Lerner Publications Company
Minneapolis

For Dorothy Rose Collins

This book is available in two editions:
Library binding by Lerner Publications Company,
 a division of Lerner Publishing Group
Soft cover by First Avenue Editions,
 an imprint of Lerner Publishing Group
241 First Avenue North
Minneapolis, MN 55401 U.S.A.

Website address: www.lernerbooks.com

Library of Congress Cataloging-in-Publication Data

Collins, Thomas M.
    Tony Blair / by Thomas M. Collins.
      p.   cm. — (A&E biography)
    Includes bibliographical references and index.
    ISBN: 0–8225–2373–6 (lib. bdg. : alk. paper)
    ISBN: 0–8225–9622–9 (pbk. : alk. paper)
    1. Blair, Tony, 1953– 2. Great Britain—Politics and government—
1979–1997. 3. Great Britain—Politics and government—1997– 4. Prime
ministers—Great Britain—Biography. 5. Labour Party (Great Britain)—
Biography. I. Title. II. Series: Biography (Lerner Publications
Company)
DA591.B56C65 2005
941.085'9'092—dc22   2004019765

Manufactured in the United States of America
1 2 3 4 5 6 – JR – 10 09 08 07 06 05

CONTENTS

British prime minister Tony Blair faced strong opposition as he prepared to ask the House of Commons to support war in Iraq in early 2003.

Chapter **ONE**

SUMMONS TO WAR

TUESDAY, MARCH 18, 2003. THE MORNING headlines in London, England, tell the story of the day: "George Bush Offers Saddam Hussein Exile or Destruction," "UN Pulls Out Weapons Inspectors," "France, Russia, and Germany Oppose the Use of Force."

A cold wind blows up and down tiny, tucked-away Downing Street, home of Great Britain's prime minister, Tony Blair. On this raw spring morning, he sits in a small den in his official home as he makes the final changes to the speech he is about to give. It is the most serious speech that a head of state can give—a summons to war.

Millions of Britons in all of England's major cities and other citizens in cities all over the world have been in

In early 2003, at least 750,000 people filled London's streets to protest the looming U.S.-led war in Iraq. It was the largest demonstration ever held in that city.

the streets protesting the war that many fear is to come. At times it seems that Tony Blair and George Bush, president of the United States, are the only people on the planet who are willing to go to war with Iraq. Certainly, Prime Minister Blair's own Labour Party is up in arms. While Blair is popular for winning elections for Labour, he is denounced for leading the charge to war. Three ministers have resigned from his government, and more than one hundred Labour members of Parliament are sure to vote against him on this day.

It will require every ounce of his powers of persuasion for Blair to convince enough of his Labour allies

of the need for war to win the majority vote. His tradi-
tional political enemies, the Conservatives, actually support him on this issue.

Blair had written most of the speech a few days before,
sitting in another small room upstairs, surrounded by
books on Islam (the main religion in Iraq)—and by John
Lennon CDs. The main points of his argument he can
scribble on the back of an envelope. They spring from
that terrible day in the United States—September 11,
2001—when nineteen al-Qaeda terrorists hijacked pas-
senger airplanes and crashed them into the twin towers
of the World Trade Center in New York and the Pentagon in Washington, D.C., launching a global conflict of a
kind the world had never known before.

Blair outlined his main points:

- Saddam Hussein, the leader of Iraq, was a past,
  present, and future threat. Blair and former
  U.S. president Bill Clinton had controlled his
  actions for years with air strikes against Iraqi
  military targets.
- The United States and Great Britain were
  among Saddam's enemies.
- The people of the United States were ready to
  follow President Bush into war against Saddam.
  It was going to happen regardless of what anyone did or said.
- The people of Great Britain and the rest of
  Europe would not support the United States

unless the United Nations—an international body set up after World War II (1939–1945) to promote world peace—played an important role in the process.

- And finally, it would be better for the world if the United States had international support and did not go to war alone.

These were the reasons the stakes were so high. Yet, while the aims of the two world leaders, Bush and Blair, seemed the same, they were quite different. The Bush administration was focusing on the removal of Saddam from power in Iraq. Blair was committed to using military power to create a world based on international cooperation, not war. The power would be

Saddam Hussein, left, longtime leader of Iraq, was seen by the United States as a threat to world security.

used to encourage nations to work together for the betterment of all communities and individuals. Somehow, Prime Minister Blair has to make this clear to the House of Commons and to the U.S. president.

On March 18, 2003, Blair steps into the chamber of the House of Commons and takes his place in the front row of the Labour benches facing the opposition, the Conservatives. It is two o'clock in the afternoon. The room is jammed, and the air charged with electricity and deep emotion. Tony Blair readies himself for his moment in history. As he rises, the fate of nations—and of innocent individuals—hangs in the balance.

The Blair family in 1956, from left to right, *Hazel, William, Tony, and Leo*

Chapter **TWO**

A MIDDLE-CLASS CHILDHOOD

ANTHONY CHARLES LYNTON (TONY) BLAIR WAS born early on the morning of May 6, 1953, in Edinburgh, Scotland. He was the second child and second son of Leo and Hazel Blair.

Leo Blair had been raised by foster parents, shipyard worker James Blair and his wife, Mary, in working-class Glasgow, Scotland. His birth parents were young actors unable to care for him.

Leo Blair joined the army in 1942 and rose to the rank of lieutenant. In 1948 he married Hazel Corscaden from Ballyshannon, Ireland. Their first child William was born in 1950.

At the time of Tony's birth, his father was a tax official. At night Leo studied law at Edinburgh

University. Soon after, he accepted a position as a lecturer in law at the University of Adelaide in Australia and moved his family halfway around the world.

During the monthlong ocean voyage, Tony displayed some of the charm that he would become famous for. Much to the delight of the passengers and the ship's band, the toddler did a little dance wearing only his diaper. Leo Blair recalled, "The dance ended only when his nappy [diaper] dropped to his ankles."

The Blairs lived in Adelaide for three and a half years. It was a very happy time for the family. The Blair family's third child, Sarah, was born there.

In January 1958, the family returned to Great Britain. Tony's father had taken a position as a law lecturer at Durham University in Durham, England, an old cathedral city 250 miles northwest of London. Leo Blair lectured at the university and started his own private law practice as a barrister (in Great Britain, a lawyer who appears in court) in the nearby town of Newcastle upon Tyne.

One reason Leo Blair wanted to return to England was to run for a seat in Parliament as a member of the Conservative Party. As son William remembers, "From the time we came back to Britain, our father was politically ambitious. He was a good communicator, and had a flair for making his ideas interesting."

Tony's mother liked nothing more than being surrounded by her family. As a child, Tony spent part

Durham, England, in the late 1930s. Durham Cathedral and Durham Castle can be seen in the background, just past Framwellgate Bridge.

of every summer with the rest of the Blair family in Ireland in his mother's hometown.

"We had a perfectly good, average, middle-class standard of living," Tony once told an interviewer. Actually, Leo Blair made a good salary as a university professor. With his successful private law practice, the Blairs lived a very comfortable and perhaps above average middle-class life.

In 1961, when he was eight, Tony followed his older brother William to Chorister School, a private school affiliated with Durham's cathedral. He immediately became known as Blair Two and was smart enough to skip the lowest grade.

Tony was a good athlete and was interested in sports, particularly football (called soccer in the United States). Later, Tony played on the school cricket and rugby teams, and in his final year, he was named the school's best rugby player.

Tony loved to read too. "As a boy I read avidly," he told the *Times* of London on World Book Day, April 23, 1998. "C. S. Lewis's Narnia adventures, . . . Denis Wheatley's war books, and Robert Louis Stevenson's *Kidnapped*. But I enjoyed most the world created by Tolkien in *The Lord of the Rings*."

The headmaster of Chorister School, Canon John Grove, remembers Tony with "a perpetual, almost impish" smile on his face. But the Blairs were strict about manners, and Blair Two and his brother Bill were polite and well behaved.

Tony recalled, "They always said, 'Misbehave inside the family if you will, but outside make us proud of you.' Respect for others, courtesy, giving up your seat for the elderly, saying please and thank you. . . . If I was told off [scolded] at school, I was told off again at home. When my mother saw the teacher, she apologised for me."

With a secure teaching position, a thriving legal practice, and a budding political career, Leo Blair was able to move the family into a big new house a few miles outside Durham. They even owned an automobile, something very few middle-class people could afford at the time. In 1964, only six years after arriving in Durham, Leo Blair was the head of the local Conservative Party group.

END OF CHILDHOOD

Tony Blair recalled it as "the day my childhood ended." Early in the morning of July 4, 1964, Tony's mother came to his room and woke him. "A child gets an immediate sense of when something terrible has happened. My mother hadn't even spoken and I was in tears. Then she said, 'Daddy's not very well, something happened in the night,' and I knew it was dreadful and serious."

Only forty years old, Leo Blair had suffered a severe stroke in the middle of the night. He was unable to speak and was partially paralyzed.

All day long, Blair hovered between life and death as Tony's mother kept a vigil at his hospital bedside. By late afternoon, they knew Leo Blair would live. But he was unable to walk, and more seriously, he had completely lost the power of speech.

The family was devastated. Everything had been going so well, then in an instant, it was gone, changed forever. The experience was Tony's introduction to the facts of life: things could go well, and they could go badly. It also taught him about commitment and love as he watched his mother nurse his father back to health.

With his wife's dedication and loving help, Leo Blair was out of bed and walking within a few months. But

Hazel Blair worked with her husband for three long years before he could speak properly again. William was away at Fettes College boarding school, and Tony seemed to bear more than his share of responsibility.

But more trouble lay ahead. As Leo Blair was recuperating, eight-year-old Sarah became ill with Still's disease, a form of arthritis that afflicts mainly young people.

"My sister was in hospital for two years, as they treated the illness quite differently then," said Tony later. "It was a terrible thing because she had to have all sorts of drugs. My mum was coping with that and my dad at the same time and she was an absolute rock."

Twelve-year-old Tony, left, and his brother Bill, right

In the spring of 1966, the Chorister School held a mock election. No doubt under the influence of his father's political views, twelve-year-old Tony was the Conservative candidate. However, on the day of the election, Tony was ill. Another boy took his place and easily won. Tony's first political campaign was his last as a member of the Conservative Party.

Fettes College, where Tony attended high school, admitted its first students in 1870.

Chapter **THREE**

FETTES, OXFORD, AND ROCK AND ROLL

AFTER CHORISTER SCHOOL, TONY FOLLOWED HIS brother to Fettes College, outside of Edinburgh, for his high school years. Fettes's most famous graduate had been the fictitious secret agent, James Bond.

Most of the new boys, like Tony, were not prepared for the harsh discipline and strict traditions at Fettes. Nik Ryden, who met Tony at Fettes, when both boys were thirteen, recalled the meeting.

"It was a cold October, it was a gray building and it was a shock to everyone, kids our age, to be lumped into this place. It was a place where you had to learn to be self-sufficient. The ethos [belief] was that you were there to maintain the [British] empire. There was a fair degree of survival of the fittest."

At Fettes, prefects (upperclassmen who had charge of the younger boys) were allowed to cane—actually hit with a cane—their charges. Each prefect had an underclassman who would act as the upperclassman's servant. The younger boy would have to do everything the prefect asked, from polishing his shoes to bringing him his toast and tea in the morning.

There were rules for everything from the length of students' hair to how many buttons to button on their coats. Tony was something of a cutup, and he was certainly caned in his first year. It is no wonder he hated the school.

Eric Anderson, a new English professor, had far more liberal ideas than most of the other teachers, and Tony was immediately drawn to him. Anderson liked the bright, impish, and cheerful young Blair and acknowledged later "there was some sort of chemistry between us."

Anderson was going to start a new house for students in Tony's second year. There would be no hierarchies, no waiting on upperclassmen, very little, if any, corporal punishment. Tony was desperate to be admitted. When selected, he happily looked forward to a better experience in the fall.

Before beginning his second year, however, Tony seems to have had second thoughts. He boarded the train for Edinburgh and waved good-bye to his parents. Then he walked the length of the train, got off at the end, and jumped on a train for the Newcastle airport. He decided he would fly to the Bahamas, instead.

Somehow Tony actually managed to board an airplane before he was discovered without a boarding pass. By the time he was finally hand-delivered to school by his parents, he was in a good deal of trouble with them and the headmaster.

Even so, Tony was a good student. He excelled in Latin and Scriptures (Bible study) and was a member of the debating society. He was a good athlete too, especially at ball sports such as rugby, cricket, and, unusual in Great Britain, basketball.

Tony was famous for his pranks and for teasing his fellow schoolmates. The pranks, his sloppy clothes, and rule breaking continued to land him in trouble. One classmate recalled, "His tie was always slightly undone, he had dirty shoes, he was questioning things the whole time. He was an extremely annoying character for a lot of people."

Professor Anderson certainly knew from firsthand experience how exasperating young Blair could be. "I got used to a knock at my door, followed by the grinning Blair's face and a fifteen minute argument about some way of doing things which the school ought, he thought, to change at once. Tony was full of life, maddening at times, pretty full of himself and very argumentative. He was an expert at testing rules to the limit. . . . I was always telling him to get his hair cut and to pull up his tie. But he was a live wire and fun to have around."

REBELLIOUS TIMES

The 1960s were a time when rebellion, even revolution, was in the air—in music, politics, all areas of life. Riots, student demonstrations against the war in Vietnam (1954–1975), a civil rights movement in the United States, and even the first man to land on the moon happened during this era.

"The times they are a-changin'," as American musician Bob Dylan sang. The old way of doing things did not seem to be relevant any longer.

Tony was, like many other people, infected with the spirit of the times. He left compulsory military training at Fettes and opted for alternative service instead. The alternative service meant working among the poor and elderly in a slum area of Edinburgh for the next two years.

Nik Ryden remembers, "We were there [at Fettes] when the world was changing in a big way. It felt like you were stuck in this place and you could have been anywhere. Students were rioting, there was the change in music, and we were sitting there doing our Latin and going to chapel twice a day and playing at being a soldier on Wednesday afternoons."

Eventually, Tony's restless spirit found a natural outlet in performing. At Fettes, he played Marc Antony in Shakespeare's *Julius Caesar*. Tony and a few friends started their own drama company and staged plays by new British playwrights such as Harold Pinter and Tom Stoppard.

Ryden remembers, "Tony was very keen on debating and acting. If you ask me if there were signs of what he was going to become then I would say no, but there was the acting and debating, skills that are vital for any successful politician. He is sincere and he is genuinely caring but also there is this actor ability. Even if someone were boring the pants off him, he would still appear interested. That is one of the tricks."

Neither his tongue nor his agile mind, however, could save Tony from the humiliating experience that befell him in his final year at Fettes. His friend, benefactor, and teacher, Eric Anderson, left Fettes that year. The new headmaster of the house found Tony, "the most difficult boy I ever had to deal with." For general insubordination (disobedience) and breaking school rules, Tony's new headmaster gave him "six of the best" (six of the hardest blows he could administer with the cane). It was almost unheard of, even at Fettes, that a seventeen-year-old upperclassman would be beaten. Tony spent the last part of his final year living in exile from the school at a friend's parents' house nearby.

ROCK-AND-ROLL YEAR

Tony wanted to follow brother William to Oxford to read (study) law. Rather than go directly there, though, he decided to take a year off. He headed to London to seek his fortune in popular music.

Tony showed up on the doorstep of a friend of a friend, Alan Colenette, who was trying to promote rock-and-roll bands. The bands were made up of schoolboys having fun before they buckled down to university and business. Alan recalled, "His belongings consisted of a home-made blue guitar which he called 'Clarence,' from which the entire neck would separate during rapid riffs, and a tatty brown suitcase containing a maximum of one change of clothes."

Alan and Tony joined forces to discover and promote the next Rolling Stones or Led Zeppelin. Tony brought energy, a sense of drive, and optimism to the enterprise. They put together a band, and Tony found a local church with a kind of youth club where young people could socialize.

Alan and Tony bought an old run-down blue Ford van to drive their bands to gigs around London and outlying areas. Late one night, the van went careering through London with Tony at the wheel. As he skidded around a corner, he lost control and sideswiped a new Jaguar parked along the street. Everyone in the van told him to drive on. The owner of the Jaguar would never know. Tony pulled over and left a note of apology, with his phone number and a promise to pay for the damages. The band shared the cost of the repairs.

Tony wasn't a great rock-and-roll performer or manager, but he certainly dressed like one. He always played up his resemblance to Mick Jagger of the Rolling Stones, with hair past his shoulders and outfits almost as outrageous—tight, white, lace-up bell-bottom pants, striped school blazers, and an oversized brown fur coat.

The end of Tony's and Alan's rock-and-roll promotion careers occurred on Tony's nineteenth birthday, May 6, 1972. That night they put on a concert with a number of bands in a very large hall. No one came. The next night was only a little better, but it was the end.

Despite the failure of their enterprise, it had been great fun. As one friend said about Tony, "His tremendous enthusiasm even then was overwhelming. He was extremely determined and able to work much harder than anyone else I knew."

Rock-and-roll Tony in the late 1970s

SAINT JOHN'S COLLEGE

Tony finally entered Saint John's College, Oxford, in the early summer of 1972. His friends thought that he was becoming more serious, but he was still an attention-grabbing rebel.

Tony had never been particularly interested in politics or religion, but that changed soon after entering the university. As he said many years later, "My Christianity and my politics came together at the same time." That time was in his first year at Oxford, when he met the man he was to call "the person who most influenced me."

Peter Thomson was a charismatic, thirty-six-year-old student from Australia. A self-described "renegade priest" of the Anglican (English Protestant) Church, Thomson was earning a degree in theology. He and a group of other students, including Tony, had conversations about life and politics that lasted all night. Tony was inspired by the ideas of social and economic justice, social responsibility, and the importance of making a difference that came out of these discussions.

Thomson introduced Tony and the others to the philosophy of John Macmurray and the idea of "Community." The Scottish-born Macmurray was a teacher and a popular philosopher on British Broadcasting Corporation (BBC) radio in the 1930s. He taught that by doing good works for the whole community, people helped the individuals in it and helped themselves. This became the core of Tony's philosophy of life and governing. As he said many years later when he was elected Labour leader, "If you really want to understand what I am all about, you have to take a look at a guy called John Macmurray. It's all there."

Thomson returned to Australia at the end of Tony's second year at Oxford, but he had left an indelible mark upon the young man. Tony later explained, "I had always believed in God but . . . Peter made it relevant, practical rather than theological. Religion became less of a personal relationship with God. I began to see it in a much more social context."

At the end of his second year, Tony was confirmed into the Church of England. One of the few friends who even knew about it recalls that Tony also considered entering the ministry. However serious his political and religious interests were becoming, Tony hadn't lost his interest in cutting up, acting out, or rock and roll.

At about the same time, an Oxford band called the Ugly Rumors (the name came from the cover of a Grateful Dead album) needed a lead singer. Mark Ellen, the band's bass player, remembered, "I had joined this band with a couple of friends and we knew we weren't going to get anywhere without a front man." Someone had seen Tony in a review at Saint John's College, and they asked him to join the band. Tony said, "Great, what songs do you do?"

Not only was Tony good, he showed up prepared. Mark Ellen remembered, "He was fantastically confident but without any arrogance or swagger. He had ambition, enormous charm. He even wanted to rehearse. He said to me: 'What's the point of doing it if we can't be good?' "

Their first gig turned into a near farce. As the band churned out a beat, Tony jumped onstage in a perfect Mick Jagger impersonation, finger-wagging and dancing in cutoff T-shirt and purple bell-bottoms.

Right in the middle of the third song, the drums fell apart with a resounding crash, and the song came to a stuttering halt. Without missing a beat, as if he'd been onstage and doing this all his life, Tony grabbed the microphone and entertained the crowd while the band put the drum set back together.

"He held the entire thing together and we were just amazed. And he was really funny and charming, . . . I can remember standing there in the back line with my bass guitar, . . . looking at him and thinking: *'this is no ordinary junior love-god lead singer we have here. Where is this guy going to go?'* "

Even while a member of the band, Tony was able to keep up with his studies too. But as he took his final examinations at Oxford, his mother fell ill. She had been diagnosed with cancer five years before, and she had a severe relapse.

Two weeks after Tony graduated, Hazel Blair, fifty-two, died. His mother had always been the real strength of the family. Peter Thomson, who was with the family at the time of Hazel Blair's death, said, "It was absolutely clear that she doted on Tony and that Tony adored her. She also had a deep social conscience and I think Tony has turned out to be the type of human being that she would have wanted him to be."

Tony later said that, when his mother died, he realized "that life is finite, so if you want to get things done you had better get a move on. . . . My life took on an urgency which has probably never left it."

Blair was an excellent barrister (lawyer), but he had greater ambitions.

Chapter **FOUR**

THE LAW
AND POLITICS

BEFORE BECOMING PRACTICING BARRISTERS, LAW graduates in Great Britain intern at law firms. As interns they study for the bar examination, an exam lawyers must pass in order to legally practice in their field.

Blair moved to London and applied for an internship with an influential barrister, Alexander Irvine. Irvine had already taken on a brilliant student, a young woman named Cherie Booth. Cherie had just graduated with the highest honors from the prestigious London School of Economics. Irvine judged her to be the smarter of the two applicants. But something about Blair's enthusiasm and his charm convinced Irvine to find a place for him too.

Irvine's suspicions about who was the better student

were confirmed when Booth took a first in the bar exams and Blair took an undistinguished third. It didn't seem to bother Blair much. He headed off to France, where he tended bar in a Paris hotel. At the end of the summer, he bicycled through France.

When he finally returned to London, he joined his fellow pupil, Booth, already hard at work in Irvine's office. Working together, Booth and Blair struck up a warm friendship. As Blair remembered, "In the first bit of the pupillage [internship], I was struggling a bit. . . . She helped me enormously."

Not long after that, Blair and Booth started going out together. Both were intelligent, ambitious, young, soon-to-be-successful lawyers. And they were in love.

Cherie Booth and Tony Blair had come from very different backgrounds. Blair's upbringing had been stable and emotionally and financially secure. Booth, on the other hand, had known real hardship and struggle. Her father had abandoned the family when Cherie was nine years old. But Cherie shone as a student at her local convent school and was promoted a year ahead of her age group. By hard work and persistence, she won scholarships to pay for her education.

Cherie joined the Socialist Party at the age of sixteen. As a teenager, she announced, "I want to be Britain's first female prime minister." In fact, after Booth and Blair started dating, most of their friends thought that she would have a great political career and that he would be a successful lawyer.

Margaret Thatcher was a member of Britain's Conservative Party. She was prime minister from 1979 to 1990, becoming Britain's longest serving prime minister in more than 150 years.

When Margaret Thatcher became Britain's first female prime minister in 1979, Blair and Booth had been going out for a couple of years. Blair proposed to Booth that summer during a vacation in the Tuscany region of Italy.

On March 29, 1980, Tony Blair and Cherie Booth were married in the chapel of Saint John's College, Oxford. Blair was offered a permanent position with Irvine practicing employment law for both employers and trade unions. He was a very good lawyer as it turned out. Irvine remembers that he "was very good at getting to the point. He was a fast gun on paper, possessing an excellent facility with the English language."

Booth and Blair became involved in their local branch of the Labour Party. A vague desire in Blair began to grow into a strong idea. He wanted to go into politics and stand for a seat in Parliament.

THE BRITISH SYSTEM OF GOVERNMENT

Britain's form of government is a parliamentary democracy. The government is run by a legislature, with a constitutional monarch (king or queen) as head of state, somewhat like the U.S. president. (The modern monarch is Queen Elizabeth II. Her oldest son, Charles, would become king upon her death. His sons with his wife, Princess Diana, are William and Harry.)

Britain's legislature is called Parliament. It includes the House of Commons, the House of Lords, and the king or queen. The House of Commons, or Commons, is made up of 651 elected members of Parliament (MPs), who represent local voting districts. The House of Lords is made up of 1,185 lords and ladies—most of whom have inherited their titles—and the two archbishops and the twenty-four most senior bishops of the Church of England.

The real power in Parliament lies in the House of Commons. General elections to choose MPs must be held at least every five years. The government is formed by the party with a majority of seats in the House of Commons. The queen appoints the party's leader as prime minister. As head of the government, the prime minister appoints about one hundred ministers. About twenty ministers make up the cabinet, the senior group that advises the prime minister. The second largest party forms the official Opposition. The Opposition has a duty to challenge government policies and to present an alternative program.

The House of Commons can force the government formed by the party in power to resign by passing a resolution of no confidence. The government must also resign if Commons rejects a proposal vital to its policies. When this happens, new elections must be held.

The Blairs made a family deal: whoever made it to Parliament first would have the full support of the other.

RUNNING FOR PARLIAMENT

When the Conservative member of Parliament from Beaconsfield (a town north of London) died in February 1982, Tony Blair seized the opportunity to make a run for the seat. He was articulate, energetic, and charming, and people liked him. But if there was one seat in Great Britain that the Conservative candidate was sure to win, it was Beaconsfield's.

It was a hopeless cause, and Blair lost handily. Even so, the young Blair had caught the attention of the

Blair energetically campaigned for the Beaconsfield Parliament seat in 1982.

Labour Party leadership. On election night, one Labour leader appearing on television news said, "We believe he's going to have a very big future in British politics."

Blair continued to work in Alexander Irvine's law practice, but he also wrote political articles for London journals and looked for another opportunity to run for Parliament. Then in March 1983, the new voting district of Sedgefield was created near Durham, Blair's hometown. This was solid Labour territory, the home of miners and other working-class people. Whoever could win the Labour Party nomination for the new seat was almost guaranteed to be elected. It would be a safe seat for Labour.

Blair's hopes rose. On May 9, only a few days after Blair's thirtieth birthday, Prime Minister Thatcher announced a general election would be held in one month, on June 9, 1983.

RUNNING AGAIN

Blair found out that Trimdon Village hadn't yet nominated a candidate, and two days after the election announcement, Blair called John Burton, the secretary of the Trimdon Village branch of the new Sedgefield Labour district. Each branch could nominate a candidate for the seat.

When Blair asked to meet with the Trimdon branch, Burton invited him to an informal meeting of branch members that night. The first item on the agenda was an important football match on the telly (television).

The match ran into overtime, and finally, hours after Blair had arrived, the men got around to interviewing him. Blair talked about his ideas for widening the base of the Labour Party. He also told them he disagreed with Labour policy regarding Europe. The Labour Party was not in favor of Britain's membership in the European Economic Community (a political and economic organization of European countries that is now known as the European Union, or EU). Blair thought that Britain should play a greater role in European affairs and that the future lay in cooperation among European countries.

Burton had thought of seeking the nomination for himself. But he later said, "As soon as I met Tony, anyway, I knew that he was the chap [man] and not myself. That he was better able to take the party forward and change the party than I would be."

Blair won the men's endorsement that night, and they became known as the "Famous Five," the five men who started Blair in politics. Their endorsement was crucial, but it was only the first step in getting the nomination.

The election campaign was already under way when the Sedgefield Labour Party finally nominated Tony Blair. With only a few weeks to go before the general election, Blair was off and running.

The general election of 1983 was a disaster for Labour. They won only 28 percent of the vote and lost more seats in Parliament than any time since 1940.

Blair presents the Labour Party's National Award of Merit to Jack Oldham, a member of the Labour Party for sixty years, during the 1983 Sedgefield campaign.

But their candidate in Sedgefield won by more than eight thousand votes. At the age of thirty, Anthony Charles Lynton Blair was on his way as Labour's youngest member of Parliament.

SEEDS OF FUTURE REFORM

As he had campaigned for his seat, the newly elected Labour MP from Sedgefield had noticed how popular Prime Minister Thatcher—a Conservative—was even among Labour voters. Thatcher had been elected in 1979 because the voters had become dissatisfied with Labour's policies. Blair knew why she was popular. He could recall as a child hearing his Conservative father say, "Labour holds you back. It doesn't want you to succeed. It doesn't want you to do well." Thatcher was seen as the champion of the individual and of people's dreams for a better life.

In the 1983 election, Labour had proposed extreme left-wing policies, such as withdrawal from the European Economic Community and unilateral (without the cooperation of other countries) nuclear disarmament. Blair opposed both those policies. He believed that if he and the Labour Party were to have a future, he would have to work to change the party's philosophy, its policies, and the way it presented itself to voters. Blair knew that Labour needed to be seen as working for the individual, for smart government, not big government, and for wise economic policies, not just more new taxes. He decided that this would be his project as a member of Parliament and of the party.

BLAIR AND BROWN

In June 1983, newly elected MP Tony Blair went to Westminster, the section of London where the British government buildings are. He was assigned to share an office—no more than a large closet tucked behind a corridor in the House of Commons—with another new Labour MP, Gordon Brown. They immediately recognized each other as allies, and they often discussed how they could change the party. To do so, the two new young MPs would face a century of tradition, history, and old-time politicians.

Gordon Brown, left, was a college chaplin and lecturer before becoming an MP in 1983.

The men were a study in contrasts. Brown, two years older than Blair, was also from Scotland but from a different social class (an important fact of British life). Tony was middle class and educated in private schools, while Brown had never gone to a school requiring tuition.

In addition, Blair was a novice in politics and had come to the Labour Party just recently. He seemed to have lucked into a safe seat. Brown had joined the party when he was a teen and had risen in the ranks. Becoming a member of Parliament was the fulfillment—almost—of his lifelong, hard-sought ambition.

The two men could not have looked and acted more differently either. Blair was tall, fair, and charming, with an easy smile. Brown was stocky—like the rugby player he had once been—dark, intense, frowning, with rough edges. Both men were hard workers. Tony was solid and focused and could apply himself. But no one could rival Brown for working day and night and studying the ins and outs of government.

"Brown and Blair" as they came to be known, were a perfect match, perhaps because of their differences. While Blair was excellent at presenting the ideas and positions with his smooth manner and smile, Brown knew how the government worked and how to work with it. Brown taught Blair where the real powers resided inside government and how to play the politics game. Blair was a quick learner and had a sharp mind, Brown thought. Brown was also impressed with Blair's ability to get to the heart of an issue and make powerful, persuasive arguments. In a short time, the men had become equal partners in the most powerful alliance in British politics since the end of World War II (1939–1945).

In the heated debates on the floor of the House of Commons, Blair proved to be quick on his feet and with his brain and tongue. He wasn't as forceful as Brown, perhaps, but he made friends, not enemies—a great asset for an aspiring politician.

Still, Blair was something of an outsider. Unlike the vast majority of Labour members, he had attended private school and he wasn't consumed by politics. He didn't network in the pubs (bars) or at the clubs after hours. He preferred to get home to his wife—and to their children. Euan was born in January 1984 and Nicholas in December 1985. In blue jeans, open shirt, strumming a guitar, Tony Blair seemed very ordinary.

Blair was very much a media person. His youthful manner and natural performing talent were perfect for television, radio, and newspapers. Soon he was being interviewed and being noticed, not only in the Labour Party but also more widely through the press. Blair was surely one of the first Labour politicians in history to seek out the media. Labourites often distrusted the press, believing it favored the Conservatives.

SHADOW CABINET

In the British political system, every member of the cabinet (the chief advisers in government) has a counterpart (the shadow cabinet) in the main party out of power. Blair rose to be spokesman for the shadow trade and industry secretary.

During those first three years, Brown and Blair pushed for the modernization of the party. They worked on each other's speeches and on articles that sharpened their vision of what the new party should be. They also sharpened their attacks on the Thatcher government.

In 1985 Labour Party leader Neil Kinnock hired a

young television producer, Peter Mandelson, to be the party's communications director. Mandelson joined Brown and Blair in their project. He made sure that Brown and Blair got on television and in the newspapers to deliver their message.

Going into the 1987 general election, the Labour Party had a fresh way of presenting itself, thanks to Mandelson, Brown, and Blair. But the party as a whole preferred to stay with familiar people and ideas and with the same basic positions on defense and the economy as in 1983. It was not surprising that the Conservatives once again won a large majority in the House of Commons. Perhaps Prime Minister Margaret Thatcher and her policies were too popular to overcome.

Despite a stinging defeat for Labour, there was cause for hope. The loss was not as bad as in 1983, and the nucleus for (core of) the revolution of New Labour was in place.

After the general election, Brown was elected to the shadow cabinet as chief secretary, and Blair was appointed deputy to the shadow secretary of trade and industry. Blair worked hard and built support among Labour MPs. He became more of an insider. He wrote a semi-regular column in the influential newspaper, the *Times* of London. This put his ideas and his name in front of the public. In December 1987, the Blairs celebrated the birth of their first daughter, Kathryn.

Blair at home with his three children, from left to right, *Euan, Kathryn, and Nicholas*

In November 1988, Blair was appointed to the shadow cabinet as energy secretary. In October 1989, he became shadow employment secretary. As Blair moved smoothly up the Labour ladder, Margaret Thatcher was slipping from power.

The economic boom during the Conservative years in power was disappearing at the end of the 1980s. Interest rates soared, unemployment grew, and the economy slumped into a recession. When Thatcher proposed a new tax, it provoked protests all over England and Wales. One million people marched in London's streets.

The Conservatives could sense an impending electoral defeat, and the formerly invincible Thatcher became unpopular even in her own party. On November 27, 1990, she was replaced by John Major. At last, it looked as if the Labour Party might win an election. The Conservatives seemed to have lost their way, and John Major was not a popular candidate.

Kinnock supported the pace of modernization and reform going on in the Labour Party, but it still wasn't fast or deep enough. When John Major called a general election for April 9, 1992, Labour lost again. The Conservatives were down to a small, twenty-one-seat majority, but it was a majority nonetheless.

In the early 1990s, Blair pushed for reform in the Labour Party.

Chapter **FIVE**

FROM THE SHADOWS TO LEADER

IMMEDIATELY AFTER THE LOSS, BLAIR GAVE A SHARP assessment of the result: "The true reason for our defeat is not complex. It is simple. It has been the same since 1979. Labour has not been trusted to fulfill the aspirations [hopes] of the majority of the people in a modern world."

As shadow employment secretary, Blair had pushed reform to the limit. He even supported "open shops"— where workers could choose whether or not to join a union. Traditionally, the Labour Party and the unions endorsed a closed-shop policy. Workers in certain industries and trades were required to join the union.

Blair thought it was time to push hard to modernize the party. After the election and the surprising results, Kinnock stepped down as leader of Labour. Gordon Brown refused to go after the position. Instead, Kinnock was replaced by John Smith, one of Labour's old-timers. Smith selected Brown to be shadow chancellor and Blair as shadow home secretary (the equivalent of attorney general in the United States). At thirty-nine years old, Tony Blair had risen to the third highest post in the Labour Party. The modernizers had won everything but the Labour Party leadership.

LESSONS FROM CLINTON AND THE CONSERVATIVES

In spite of his personal success, Blair was frustrated at the slow pace of change. Then, in the fall of 1992, Blair and Labour were offered a striking example of how to win back power. In the United States, a young Arkansas governor, Bill Clinton, was elected the first Democratic president since Jimmy Carter in 1976. He did so by attracting mainstream voters who were not necessarily Democrats. The strategy was simple—the voters in the center decided elections. Win them over, and you've won the election.

In the first week of 1993, Brown and Blair visited Washington, D.C. They met with some of Clinton's chief advisers and heard and saw how the Clinton campaign had fashioned a new coalition of voters to win. Clinton's philosophy placed personal responsibility at the center.

Over the years, both the Democratic and Labour parties had promoted a sense of entitlement, the feeling that the government owed the individual something. There had been little emphasis on what the individual owed the larger community. As President John F. Kennedy had said years before, "Ask not what your country can do for you; ask what you can do for your country."

Brown and Blair could see the obvious lessons, and it confirmed many of Blair's beliefs. Conservatives saw big government as an obstacle to individual freedom and advancement. Labour saw government as the protector and helper of the individual. Blair realized that Labour needed to reclaim from the Conservatives the issues of "Community" and individual responsibility. The old dividing lines between right and left, liberal and conservative were becoming less important to voters. What were important were policies that advanced the hopes and dreams and desires of individual people and of society as a whole.

Three days after returning from Washington, Blair, in a radio interview, said, "I think it's important that we are tough on crime and tough on the causes of crime, too." Labour always seemed more concerned with explaining criminal behavior by pointing to poverty, a lack of education, and other disadvantages. Here was Blair demanding that criminals, as well as society, take responsibility.

One month later, the British were shocked and horrified by the random, brutal murder of two-year-old

James Bulger by two ten-year-old boys. As Labour
spokesman for the issue, Blair spoke out harshly. He
said, "We cannot exist in a moral vacuum. If we do
not learn and then teach the value of what is right
and what is wrong the result is simply moral chaos
which engulfs us all." Blair had taken the issue of law
and order away from the Conservatives and made it
part of the Labour agenda. Suddenly, he was seen as
someone who could bring Labour back to power.

TWISTS OF FATE AND DESTINY

On May 12, 1994, Labour's leader, John Smith, suffered a sudden and massive heart attack. At first,
Blair was certain that the new leader of Labour would
be Gordon Brown. But over the last two years, while
Brown had served as shadow chancellor, Blair, as
home secretary, had vaulted past him in the eyes of
the press, the public, and his peers. He had effectively
criticized the Conservative Party and projected the
ideas of a new Labour Party to the public.

A slow, sure wave of support began to grow in favor
of Blair. He was nice and charming, with a light, easy
touch. He had an accomplished and beautiful wife
and three handsome children. The Labourites believed
Blair could put them back in power.

Blair decided to run for Labour leader. First, however,
Gordon Brown had to be informed. Blair and Brown
(the names were reversed now) had a private dinner at
a fashionable London restaurant, where they struck an

uneasy bargain. Blair would lead Labour and the Opposition, and Brown would be his chancellor of the exchequer (the cabinet member in charge of public funds) with sweeping authority. Brown would be something of a coequal partner with Blair running Labour. If the voters approved, Brown would become Labour leader and prime minister when Blair stepped down.

On July 21, 1994, Tony Blair was elected the fifteenth leader of the Labour Party. At forty-two, he was the youngest Labour leader ever.

THE NEW LEADER FOR NEW LABOUR

In his acceptance speech, Blair seemed to be addressing not just the Labour Party but all of Britain. "I say this to the people of this country, and most of all to our young people: join us in this crusade for change. Join us. Of course, the world can't be put to rights overnight. Of course, we must avoid foolish illusions and false promises. But there is, amongst all the hard choices and uneasy compromises that politics forces upon us, a spirit of progress throughout the ages, with which we keep faith."

At a private party, he announced he wanted nothing less than "to change the country . . . to make it a country that people are proud of again, to make this country of ours a country where EVERYONE gets the chance to succeed and get on." The simple and powerful message was equal opportunity for all and advancement based on merit.

The first Labour Party conference (similar to a U.S. political party convention) after Blair became leader was in October 1994. When party members arrived in the northern seaside resort town of Blackpool, they were greeted by big banners all over town proclaiming "New Labour!" It was no longer simply "Labour."

Meanwhile, Major had lost credibility in dealing with an economy in recession. He was forced to raise taxes—something Labour was famous for. Finally, scandals rocked the party as it was discovered that Conservative MPs had taken bribes.

On March 17, 1997, John Major asked the queen to dissolve Parliament, and a general election was

Blair speaks at the October 1994 conference in Blackpool, where the Labour Party became the New Labour Party.

called for May 1. Blair was in the race of his life, and the prospects were good. Public opinion polls showed Labour ahead by 10, even 15 percent. Blair ran a cautious, well-controlled campaign. He promised very little, so that the voters would expect the same—very little.

Britain's new prime minister poses with wife, Cherie, and children Nicholas, Kathryn, and Euan outside the prime minister's official residence at 10 Downing Street.

Chapter **SIX**

PRIME MINISTER

BY TEN O'CLOCK ON ELECTION NIGHT, THE POLLS HAD closed and the news predicted a Labour landslide. Blair watched the returns with his family in Durham. "Realizing that you are about to become Prime Minister is a very strange moment," Blair recalled later. "My dad ... was absolutely knocked out by it. He said, 'Mum would have been very proud.' But he read my mood correctly. He kept saying to me during the evening, 'You will do it well.' He understood what I was worrying about."

Blair flew back to London in the middle of the night as the prime minister-elect. In the early morning hours, he went to a rally at London's Royal Festival Hall. At five in the morning, as he made his way to the stage with Cherie and supporters, the sky brightened and the sun burst forth in a clear sky. The new prime minister looked out on the crowds and said, "A new dawn has broken has it not?"

Indeed, it had, and you could feel it in the air. By midday May 2, 1997, Tony Blair, Cherie, and their three children—Euan, thirteen; Nicholas, eleven; and Kathryn, nine—were standing outside the shiny black door with the gleaming brass knocker: Number 10 Downing Street (the prime minister's official residence).

Overnight, a political upheaval of earth-shaking proportions had occurred. In the worst electoral defeat in 150 years, the Conservatives had been turned out of power. New Labour had won 44.4 percent of the vote and 419 seats. The Conservatives had won only 31.5 percent and 165 seats. It was Labour's biggest election victory since the 1930s, and the Conservative's lowest share of the vote since 1832.

The Blairs decided that they all would move to the prime minister's official residence. Actually, they moved into the larger apartments above Numbers 11 and 12 Downing Street, normally the residence of the chancellor of the exchequer. Gordon Brown agreed to take the smaller apartment above Number 10. In full view of the world, the Blairs moved in—clothes, children's toys, electric guitar and amplifiers, shoes, and a big brass bed. The British press and public were charmed and delighted. A family with young children had not lived there since 1908.

Blair, center, front row, *poses with his new Labour Party cabinet in May 1997.*

Blair was determined to govern well in his first administration. "Call me Tony," he commanded at the first cabinet meeting. He also asked all the ministers to address each other by their first names, ending a centuries-old tradition of formality. Blair's style would be completely different in British political life.

Traditionally, cabinet secretaries ruled their own area with a relatively free hand. They would sometimes even offer policies that conflicted with those of the prime minister. Not with Prime Minister Blair. Blair held authority over his government and its ministers. He did not want challenges from people within his own administration.

Blair also broke with tradition by appointing people loyal to him to the lower levels of government too. Historically, career civil servants—able, trusted people from all parties—occupied the lower rungs of government. Blair wanted all his own people in those positions. He would keep a close eye on the information that flowed out of the center of the power—the prime minister's office.

THE LOYAL INNER CIRCLE

A loyal band of dedicated people surrounded Blair. His wife was his most intimate and trusted confidant. Gordon Brown and adviser Peter Mandelson grew to despise each other, but both were dedicated to the success of Blair's government. They were the first two people whom Blair called every morning.

Brown would have broad and sweeping powers. Not only would he be the most powerful chancellor of the exchequer in the history of Great Britain, but he would also oversee the two departments of employment welfare and trade and industry. Brown ran his departments efficiently and with confidence. Nothing was proposed or done in the Blair government unless Blair and Brown had discussed it first.

Blair needed Mandelson for his shrewd political insights and his talent as a strategist and tactician. Even more important, he needed him as a confidant and friend.

Alexander Irvine, the lawyer for whom Blair and his wife had interned, was brought in as education minister. Charles Falconer, an old friend, was a trusted aide outside of government.

Three other people were members of the inner circle. Anji Hunter had run Blair's Labour office since Labour was the Opposition party. Jonathan Powell was an intellectual and a former diplomat. He had joined the Labour Party only after meeting Blair when he visited Washington, D.C., in 1993.

The last member of the inner circle was press secretary Alistair Campbell. A former tabloid journalist, tough-talking and hard-bitten, Campbell saw politics as a kind of war. Campbell made sure that no attack from the Conservatives was left unchallenged. And he made sure every cabinet member and everyone else in the administration all said essentially the same thing about an issue and that they all said it at the same time. No matter what the private feelings were in this close-knit group, all were devoted to the success of Tony Blair.

New substance came to New Labour and a new style to British government as well. The apartments on Downing Street glittered with parties full of the hip and famous. Artists, rock stars, soccer stars, writers, and movie stars flocked to Downing Street. "Cool Britannia!" proclaimed the cover of *Newsweek* magazine.

THE IRISH QUESTION

Only one week after becoming prime minister, Blair began a whirlwind tour of international meetings. For his first state visit, he picked the most troublesome spot a British prime minister could then go: Belfast, Northern Ireland.

THE TROUBLES

The roots of the Troubles (the modern-day violence between Catholics and Protestants in Northern Ireland) lay in the 400-year English rule of Ireland. In 1608 the English went into Ireland and took the best lands from the native, Gaelic-speaking, Catholic Irish. Beginning in 1610, these lands were given to Protestant settlers from England, Wales, and Scotland. For the next 350 years, the Irish natives suffered the often harsh rule of England, though they did rise up, periodically, in futile rebellion.

As the nineteenth century progressed, the northeastern counties, known as Ulster, where most of the Protestants lived, became industrialized and provided stable employment to the population. The overwhelmingly Catholic southern Ireland remained agricultural. During the Famine of 1848, more than one million people in Ireland died of starvation when the potato crop failed. Then, toward the end of the nineteenth century, the British government began to look favorably on the demands of the Irish for home rule, meaning the Irish could work out their own future for Ireland. But Ulster Unionists, Protestants who wanted to remain tied to Britain, feared that giving the Irish Catholics home rule would mean that Unionists would be ruled by the Catholic Church.

Irish nationalists rejected any compromises. They wanted Britain out of Ireland entirely. They continued to fight for independence. In May 1921, a treaty was signed that formally and legally partitioned (split) Ireland into two parts. The southern, predominantly Catholic twenty-six counties were given independence as the Republic of Ireland within the British Empire; the predominantly Protestant, English-speaking six counties of Ulster, closely tied to Britain, became part of the United Kingdom of Great Britain and Northern Ireland.

Pro-British Unionists crowded into Ulster after the partition. Still, they felt threatened by the large Catholic minority in Ulster and an independent Ireland to the south, which claimed the six counties as rightfully part of Ireland. Under this threat, the Ulster government denied civil liberties and human rights to the Catholic minority.

For nearly forty years, the IRA (the Irish Republican Army, a group dedicated to returning Ulster to Ireland) and Ulster Unionists engaged in violence and counterviolence, such as shootings and bombings. In Belfast, Northern Ireland, the two opposing sides hurled taunts, bricks, and Molotov cocktails over the walls and barbed wire that separated them. British soldiers patrolled the streets in flak jackets and armored vehicles, firing rubber bullets and tear gas at stone-throwing youths.

In 1967 the Northern Ireland Civil Rights Association formed to protest four decades of Unionist discrimination against Catholics. The civil rights campaign got Catholics politically involved for the first time since the formation of the Northern Ireland state. The group held nonviolent protest marches. Ulster Unionists opposed the marchers, sometimes violently.

One of the worst incidents of violence during the Troubles occurred on Bloody Sunday, January 30, 1972. On that day, a large, nonviolent march was held in the predominantly Catholic city of Londonderry, Northern Ireland. At the end of the march, in circumstances that are still debated, British soldiers shot dead fourteen men and wounded fourteen others. Various efforts by Great Britain to quell the violence had little success until Blair made the establishment of peace in Northern Ireland an important part of his plans for Great Britain.

Since the nineteenth century, the Irish Question (whether to grant independence to Northern Ireland) had plagued British monarchs and politicians. Britain had granted Irish independence in 1921 but retained political control of the six northern counties. Many of Ireland's Protestant minority moved there, and the six counties became known as Northern Ireland. The Catholics and Protestants of Northern Ireland grew into two bitterly divided communities. In the 1960s, fighting sprang up between the two groups and has occasionally flared up into bombings and violence.

Rioters throw stones in the streets of Belfast, Northern Ireland, in the 1960s, when violence between Irish Catholic and Protestant groups was at its peak.

Blair surprised everyone by his personal and political commitment to solving the difficult issues in Northern Ireland. In Belfast, Northern Ireland, he offered a balanced proposal. If the Irish Republican Army (IRA) would promise to end its violent attempts to drive the British out of Northern Ireland, the IRA would be asked to join the groups involved in bringing about peace. Change would have to come through the ballot box and not from a bomb or the end of a gun, Blair warned.

To the Protestant Unionists, who wanted the northern counties to remain part of Great Britain, Blair promised that they would remain so, as long as the majority wanted it. But he also made clear that the peaceful expression of political views would be the only way in which change would come.

In a speech in Belfast on May 16, 1997, he directly addressed the IRA. But he could have been speaking to the Unionists as well when he said, "The settlement train is leaving, I want you on that train. But it is leaving anyway and I will not allow it to wait for you. You cannot hold the process to ransom any longer. So, end the violence now."

ALL THE WORLDS'S A STAGE

A week after his trip to Belfast, Blair traveled to Noordvijk in the Netherlands for his first European Union summit. There he talked of his idea of a new style of governing called the Third Way. By Third Way, Blair meant that a third, or middle, way always existed between any two extremes. This had become almost the signature Blair philosophy. He believed that other European governments could use the Third Way as a model for governing in their own countries, as well.

Four days later, Blair was in Paris, France, to sign a security agreement between the North Atlantic Treaty Organization (NATO) and Russia. (NATO is an organization of European countries and the United States, pledged to come to the defense of member countries). Two days after Paris, President Clinton and First Lady Hillary Rodham Clinton visited London, and the Blairs began a warm and lasting professional and personal

The Clintons and the Blairs greet the press outside 10 Downing Street during the Clintons' first visit with the Blairs in 1997.

relationship with them. A week later, Blair was in Sweden for another European conference. There he challenged the Socialist parties of Europe to take the example of New Labour and "modernise or die."

In late June, Blair attended his first meeting of the world's seven largest industrial nations, known as G7, plus Russia, in Denver, Colorado. On the way back to Britain, he stopped in New York, to address a UN conference on the environment. There Blair declared, "My three young children in London complain that I am never at home. But if there is one summit they would want me at, it is this one. They know our decisions here will have a profound effect on the world they inherit. So I speak to you not just as the new British Prime Minister, but as a father." By December, thanks to the hard work of his secretary of state for the environment, John Prescott, Blair had succeeded in getting an agreement on a treaty in Kyoto, Japan, limiting the global use of fossil fuels to help reduce global warming.

In late June, Blair met with the Chinese leadership in Hong Kong to return control of the island city to China. (In 1898 Great Britain had agreed to return Hong Kong—one of its colonies—to China within one hundred years.) Then it was back to Britain, where it was time to govern domestically. Blair was hugely popular with the people, and New Labour had a large majority in the House of Commons. Not one rival was in sight.

THE PEOPLE'S PRINCESS

Tony Blair was asleep when the phone rang at 2 A.M. on the last day of August. Princess Diana had just been gravely injured in an auto accident in Paris. At 3:30 A.M., the phone rang again. The princess was dead, and so were her boyfriend and the car's driver. (Princess Diana and Prince Charles had recently divorced.)

With the nation poised in bewildered shock, Blair went before the TV cameras. "I feel like everyone else in this country today," he began a bit shakily. "I am utterly devastated. . . . She was the people's princess and that is how she will stay, how she will remain in our hearts and our memories forever."

"The people's princess." He had found the exact phrase, the expression that captured the essence of her compassionate personality. Blair's remarks and his touching phrase seemed to steady the country, give it a sense of how to grieve for the troubled, tragic young princess.

It was also a defining moment for Blair. He fulfilled a role perhaps never before assumed by a British prime minister. Princess Diana's and Prince Charles's two sons, William and Harry, were particularly vulnerable to a ruthless press. Queen Elizabeth herself was distraught and in an awkward position. Nothing like the royal divorce—and this death—had ever taken place before. The press, ready to pounce, watched how the monarchy would react to Diana's death.

Blair used his influence to help arrange for an extra-ordinary private and public ceremony that gave the people of Great Britain a chance to mourn their princess together. Blair had saved a potentially embarrassing situation and transformed it into one of the most amazing moments in recent British history.

BACK TO NORTHERN IRELAND

Blair continued to pursue peace in Northern Ireland, perhaps because of his mother's deep ties to the country. In the fall of 1997, he became the first British prime minister since 1921 to visit and shake hands with Irish leaders. Northern Ireland Unionists screamed "traitor!" as Blair came out of the meeting. But by boldly meeting with the Irish leaders, Blair got both sides back to the bargaining table.

When he had been prime minister, John Major had asked for President Clinton's help with the Irish Question. Clinton appointed former U.S. senator George Mitchell to lead talks between the two sides and among all parties, including the Irish government.

Slowly progress was made toward peace and stability. Blair built personal relationships with the principal figures in the negotiations: Gerry Adams, representing Sinn Fein, the political section of the IRA; David Trimble, the leader of the moderate Ulster Unionist Party (UUP); and Bertie Ahern, prime minister of the Republic of Ireland. Blair moved the men closer together, personally and politically.

Blair worked diligently to restore diplomacy among Ireland's leaders, including Prime Minister Bertie Ahern, left, and Sinn Fein president Gerry Adams, right.

Mitchell and Blair had set a deadline of Easter 1998 for the parties to come to a formal agreement. To fail would be a tremendous blow. At one point, in frustration, George Mitchell commented, "People here are nice and friendly. They're just not friendly to each other. Centuries of conflict have generated hatreds that make it virtually impossible for the two communities [Catholic and Protestant] to trust each other."

Finally, on Good Friday, April 10, 1998, the historic Belfast Agreement was agreed to by the Unionists and the Irish republic. Six weeks later, a referendum (vote) was held in all of Ireland, and the Good Friday Accords, as they are known, won the overwhelming support of the people of Ireland. The accords provided a political process through which the rights of all citizens would be respected and protected.

It was Tony Blair who had the most to do with this peace. George Mitchell wrote later, "Blair possesses the elements of effective leadership in our era. He is intelligent, articulate, decisive, and photogenic." Mitchell acknowledged that Blair took a gamble in coming to Northern Ireland as there was no promise he would succeed. Most political advisers would have told Blair not to go, but he went and saw positive results.

Blair outlines some of the key objectives of the New Labour Party in a 1997 speech.

Chapter SEVEN

TROUBLES IN IRAQ AND THE BALKANS

ON **FEBRUARY 17, 1998, THE HOUSE OF** Commons approved Blair's measure to use force in Iraq, should it become necessary in the future. This measure came about because, in 1991, Prime Minister Margaret Thatcher had joined U.S. president George H. W. Bush and a broad coalition of the world's powers to drive Iraq from Kuwait.

Iraq had invaded this small neighboring country that year. The coalition easily routed the army of Iraqi leader Saddam Hussein and pushed it back across the border. Under the terms of a UN cease-fire, the U.S. and British air forces imposed two no-fly zones, areas of Iraq in which Iraqi planes were banned. One zone was in the north, where the Kurdish people lived, the other was in the south, which was predominantly Shia Muslim. Both groups had been persecuted by Saddam and were enemies of his regime. The UN agreement also required Saddam to allow UN weapons inspectors to search Iraq for evidence of missile development, weapons of mass destruction (WMD) such as chemical or biological weapons, or evidence of a nuclear program.

After the war, Saddam repeatedly denied UN access to suspected sites. Then, unpredictably, he would cooperate. He continually tested the resolve of the UN and frustrated the inspection process. In 1998, after Parliament gave Blair the approval to use force, Saddam backed down once more, but he continued to provoke crises.

FORCE AND THE THREAT OF FORCE

Meanwhile, the Balkans, an area in southeastern Europe, was erupting into ethnic and religious conflict. In 1991, after the death of the Yugoslav dictator Tito, ancient conflicts erupted among the Orthodox Christian Serbs, the Roman Catholic Croats, and the Bosnian Muslims of Yugoslavia. These conflicts splintered the formerly unified country.

Serbian president Slobidan Milosevic ordered his forces to attack Croatia and Bosnia. These forces murdered thousands of Muslim men, women, and children in Bosnia in a brutal policy of genocide known as ethnic cleansing. In August 1995, after repeated warnings, NATO carried out air and ground artillery strikes against Serbia. Finally, negotiations with Milosevic established a fragile peace.

Serbs were a minority in the Serbian province of Kosovo. Historically, it was an Albanian Muslim region, and its people had recently been demanding separation from Serbia. Milosevic, under the pretense of protecting the Serb minority, ordered his military to attack the Albanian Muslims in Kosovo.

In June 1998, a major Serbian offensive drove more than fifty thousand Kosovo Albanians from their homes, creating a humanitarian crisis. Representing the European Union, Britain sought UN approval for new NATO air strikes. But gaining that approval was unlikely because it would be vetoed (voted down) by Russia. (Russia was a strong ally of Serbia and Milosevic and is a permanent member of the UN Security Council with power to veto Security Council measures.)

Finally, after further Serb pressure in October forced more than two hundred thousand Kosovo Albanians to flee, NATO readied five hundred fighter aircraft. Milosevic backed down within hours. He allowed two thousand unarmed international observers to enter the province to ensure there were no attacks against civilians. For the moment, the pressure was off.

Meanwhile, in Iraq, Saddam had pushed the UN inspectors too far once again, accusing them of being spies. U.S. and British warplanes were on their way to attack sites in Iraq on November 14, 1998, when

Saddam backed down again and let the inspectors go back to their work. The planes were recalled.

Blair saw the immediate effectiveness of the threat of force. He observed: "When he (Saddam) finally saw, correctly, that we were ready to use force on a substantial scale, he crumbled. I hope that other countries more dubious of the use of force may now see that Saddam is moved by the credible threat of force."

Blair was very worried about other troubles in the Middle East too. He was the only world leader who supported Clinton when he launched missiles against two targets in Afghanistan and Sudan in an unsuccessful 1998 attempt to kill a shadowy figure named Osama bin Laden. Bin Laden is the head of a then little-known Islamic fundamentalist terrorist network called al-Qaeda.

In mid-December 1998, the chief UN weapons inspector, Richard Blair, reported to Clinton that Saddam was still in breach of the UN agreement. On December 16, 1998, Prime Minister Blair and Clinton both announced a joint British-U.S air strike. Operation Desert Fox was under way to attack military targets in Iraq.

Blair admitted he felt the grave responsibility of sending British servicemen and servicewomen into combat. But he and Clinton had decided that they had to use force to enforce international law.

Weeks later, Blair was in South Africa to talk with South African leader Nelson Mandela, who had been critical of the air strikes. In a speech in Cape Town on January 8, 1999, to the South African Parliament,

Blair made a case for a moral reason for going to war. He said, "People say—and I understand—you can't be self-appointed guardians of what is right and wrong. True—but when the international community agrees [to] certain objectives and then fails to implement them, those that can act, must."

The statement clearly offered a new foreign policy, one based on the right thing to do rather than just on political issues. And it immediately led Blair back into the Balkans. Milosevic had again ordered his military to drive the Kosovo Albanians from Kosovo. The military committed many atrocities, particularly against civilians and women. Throughout February and March 1999, the Serbian leader would not allow UN peacekeepers into Serbia. Finally, in late March, he was given a final ultimatum. If he did not stop the ethnic cleansing in Kosovo, NATO planes would begin bombing Belgrade, Serbia, and Serb forces.

Milosevic did not heed this warning. NATO jets began bombing Serbian air defenses on March 24, 1999. Only days after the bombing campaign started, the roads from Kosovo into neighboring Albania and Macedonia were choked with thousands—and then hundreds of thousands—of refugees fleeing the devastation.

Milosevic gambled that he could wait out the NATO air campaign. Later, Blair admitted his concern that ordering the use of British force for the second time within a year was an overuse of force. In an article in the *Sun* in early April, Blair wrote, "This is now a battle

Hundreds of thousands of ethnic Albanians fled the Serbian province of Kosovo after NATO bombings in 1999 destroyed parts of Belgrade.

of good against evil . . . it is a battle between civilization and barbarity, democracy against dictatorship."

Soon deeply disturbing images of pitiful Kosovo Albanian refugees trudging along the road in the rain and living in makeshift camps were seen on television and in newspapers around the world. The air strikes against Serbian military targets seemed only to be making the refugee problem worse.

In late April, Blair met with Clinton in the White House. Blair was convinced that the air strikes alone would not be enough to stop the atrocities. But Clinton was opposed to putting in ground combat forces, which would lead to U.S. casualties. Blair finally persuaded Clinton to publicly suggest that he was open to using ground forces to stop the killing in Kosovo. The NATO air campaign continued.

On April 24, Blair gave an important address at the Economic Club of Chicago, Illinois. In it he outlined a global vision of activist foreign relations. Regional groups of nations, such as NATO, could enforce international law without UN approval, if their actions were within the UN Charter, which outlined the rules of how countries should treat one another. He argued that when "massive flows of refugees . . . unsettle neighboring countries, then they can properly be described as threats to international peace and security." This view was a radical departure from the UN Charter, which prohibits one country from interfering in the affairs of another country.

In early May, Blair and his wife visited a camp in Macedonia for Kosovo Albanian refugees. As the people chanted, "Tony, Tony" and his wife wept, Blair said, "This is not a battle for NATO, this is not a battle for territory; this is a battle for humanity, it is a just cause, it is a rightful cause."

Finally, on June 3, 1999, after seventy-eight days of NATO bombing, Milosevic announced that he'd had enough. Serbian forces began their withdrawal from Kosovo a week later, and the air campaign was over. Blair and Clinton had shown the world that the careful use of military power in support of moral objectives could be a powerful force for good. Old wars had been fought over control of land. The new wars could and would be fought over values.

"The right thing to do" had become a constant refrain in Blair's speeches and comments. Some thought it naive and arrogant for Blair to judge what was best for the rest of the world and then to act on this judgement. Some wondered if he weren't a bit too smug and smart for his own good.

DOMESTIC LIFE AND DOMESTIC POLITICS

Along with these criticisms, Blair had made enemies at home by attempts to manage the news and to spin (control) every story coming out of the prime minister's office. One story that needed no spin or embellishment was the happy and historic news of the upcoming birth of Blair's fourth child. Leo was born on May 20, 2000. He was the first child to be born to a serving prime minister in 151 years.

Family is the cornerstone of Blair's life. Throughout his career, he has mentioned them as his motivation for everything from his championing environmental issues to his commitment to end child poverty. In many interviews and articles, he repeated phrases such as "I am not just a politician, but a father with children of my own," and children "drive you mad, but keep you sane." He even said once, "I think I function better as a politician because I lead such a normal life."

Tony and Cherie Blair pose with son Leo.

It is a modern normal life. His wife works full-time as the founding partner of a law practice that specializes in human rights cases. A nanny cares for the children. Blair's brother's family and his wife's sister and mother live close by. Even so, Blair has been much more involved in his children's lives than many other politicians.

A few months after Leo's birth, Euan, sixteen, was arrested for late-night drinking with a group of friends. Everyone could understand a little teenage revelry after exams, but the British press made much of the fact that Euan had been left to fend for himself. His father was busy working, and his mother was vacationing in Portugal. After that, Blair became more protective of his family's privacy and further restricted the British media's access to them.

However, neither the birth of Leo nor Blair's triumph on the international stage made him popular at home in Britain. His New Labour policies were modest, but the difficulty of changing modern governments, as cumbersome as dinosaurs, proved almost insurmountable. At the beginning of 2000, a great wave of economic prosperity was sweeping global markets. New digital technologies and the Internet helped fuel the economic boom in the world's largest economies, including those of France, Germany, the United States, and Great Britain.

Near the end of 2000, though, six months before the 2001 election in the United Kingdom, cracks started to appear in the Blair government. An increase in the tax on diesel and other fuels sparked the nation's truckers to stage a spontaneous strike and brought the nation to a standstill. Blair seemed stunned as the public sided with the truckers. For the first time since he had taken office, the Conservatives surged ahead in the opinion polls.

Then a few months later, a severe outbreak of foot-and-mouth disease crippled Britain's cattle industry. Entire herds of valuable cattle had to be destroyed. British television was filled with the grisly scenes of piles of burning livestock carcasses.

Blair had to postpone the May 3 elections for a month because of the outrage caused by the spread of the disease. Then, just before election day, June 7, 2001, the country was angered by a series of train derailments and collisions that highlighted the decayed state of the country's rail system and infrastructure.

Blair could look back at some major accomplishments in his four years in office. He had introduced a higher minimum wage and a series of welfare reforms that helped families, children, and the elderly.

Most important, perhaps, he had helped to establish long-awaited independent political assemblies for Scotland and Wales. This meant changing the complex, three-centuries-long constitutional agreements with these areas. Until that time, Parliament in London made laws for these members of the United Kingdom.

On election day, the turnout was the lowest since before British women had won the right to vote in 1918. But Blair and Labour won another landslide. Blair had proved that he could govern.

Blair didn't want to be known only as the man who created—with Gordon Brown and his colleagues—the New Labour Party. Great Britain's education system, the National Health Service, private business, the infrastructure of roads and rapid transit, all needed attention. The challenges of the second term were daunting but clear.

U.S. president George W. Bush and Blair are allies and friends.

Chapter EIGHT

THE WORLD CHANGES FOREVER

IN 2001 GEORGE W. BUSH, SON OF THE FORTY-first president, George H. W. Bush, became the forty-third president of the United States. It was a delicate moment for the Blairs, who were fond of the Clintons and shared their political and social values. Bush and his wife, conservative Republicans from Texas, were very different from the Clintons. But one thing was clear: the special relationship between Great Britain and the United States would remain firm.

Blair asked Clinton how he should approach the incoming president. "Be his friend," said Clinton. "Be his best friend. Be the guy he turns to."

The new president had said during his campaign that he did not agree with the Clinton-Blair ideas of foreign policy. Bush outlined a foreign policy that focused only on national interests and the pursuit of key priorities. He did not intend to use U.S. military power for missions that didn't directly involve the United States.

Blair was the first European leader to meet with Bush. At the meeting, each man sized up the other and found him acceptable. Blair, Bush declared, "had put the charm offensive on me, and it worked." He concluded, "This is a special relationship between America and Britain, and we are going to keep it that way. I can assure you that when either of us gets in a bind, there will be a friend at the end of the phone."

For his part, Blair found Bush a straightforward man of deep personal convictions and with a greater grasp of international relations than Blair at first expected. Blair felt that the relationship could and must work to their mutual advantage.

9/11/01

On September 11, 2001, Tony Blair was in a hotel in the seaside town of Brighton, England, working on a speech. He was distracted by disturbing images coming from a television set in an adjoining room. A plane had crashed into one of the towers of the World Trade Center in New York City. When Blair saw the image of a second plane slamming into its other tower, and then a third plane into the Pentagon in Washington, D.C., he knew immediately that the world had changed forever.

The prime minister quickly returned to London and convened a meeting in a secret bunker with his security staff and senior advisers to discuss the terrorist attacks. Within hours, even before Bush had returned to Washington, D.C., from a trip to Florida, Blair met the world's press. "This is not a battle between the United States and terrorism," he explained. "But between the free and democratic world and terrorism. We therefore, here in Britain, stand shoulder to shoulder with our American friends in this hour of tragedy, and we, like them, will not rest until this evil is driven from our world."

Blair's first concern was that the United States would react too quickly and unilaterally, to seek revenge. He knew of the Bush administration's distaste for alliances that limited the United States' ability to act as it wished. He foresaw that the United States might ignore the international system in a wild pursuit of the terrorists— in this case, the fundamentalist Islamic organization al-Qaeda, headed by Osama bin Laden. Blair was concerned that speedy U.S. military actions could make matters worse internationally, provoking a global conflict between Islam and Christianity, the Middle East and the West, and even Europe in opposition to the United States. He decided that he would make every effort to see that the United States worked with an international coalition in this difficult and complex time.

Blair talked with Bush by phone the day after the attacks. The president seemed open at first to Blair's advice. But as the days passed, Blair and his advisers became increasingly worried about the warlike and uncompromising words coming from President Bush and his White House advisers. When Bush invited Blair to attend the president's speech to Congress, some of Blair's advisers didn't want him to go. They felt it would seem as though he was taking orders from Bush and the United States.

But Blair knew it was the right thing to do, as he had so often said. On September 20, after a visit to Ground Zero, where the World Trade Center towers had fallen, he traveled to Washington, D.C., and listened to President Bush address the world. When the president proclaimed that the United States "has no truer friend than Great Britain," everyone rose and cheered Blair.

Behind the scenes, Blair attempted to persuade Bush that the solution was not just military. Blair's principles of community and the shared hopes of the world's nations came into focus once again.

Blair was stunned, then, when some in Bush's cabinet talked of invading Iraq. As far as Blair knew, Iraq and Saddam Hussein had nothing to do with Islamic radical Osama bin Laden or al-Qaeda. Blair insisted that the target should be Afghanistan, where al-Qaeda was based. Finally, Bush agreed, but said that Saddam Hussein's dictatorship in Iraq was a problem that must be dealt with later. Blair agreed.

THE CASE FOR RETALIATION

A month after the attacks, Blair spoke to the Labour

Party's annual congress about the need to root out terrorism by force, if necessary, in Afghanistan. For more
than a decade, a conservative Islamic group called the
Taliban had ruled the country according to its own
strict interpretation of the Quran, the holy book of
Islam. The members of the Taliban had also provided a
safe place for the training camps and headquarters of
al-Qaeda, bin Laden, and his chief lieutenants. Blair
urged that an international coalition replace the extrem-
ist Islamic government. He called for a broad coalition
of countries to band together to rebuild Afghanistan, a
poor country that had been wracked by past wars.

A memorial to the thousands of people who had died
on 9/11, he said, "can and should be greater than simply
the punishment of the guilty. It is that out of the

Taliban fighters near Kabul, the capital of Afghanistan

shadow of this evil should emerge lasting good; destruction of the machinery of terrorism wherever it is found; hope amongst all nations of a new beginning where we seek to resolve differences in a calm and ordered way; greater understanding between nations and between faiths; and above all justice and prosperity for the poor and dispossessed, so that people everywhere can see a chance of a better future through the hard work and creative power of the free citizen, not the violence and savagery of the fanatic."

AN UNEASY ALLIANCE

Throughout the fall, Blair traveled around the Middle East and the world. He called for the healing of divisions created by conflict on how to deal with the radical Taliban and al-Qaeda. He strove to be a calming influence in a troubled world. British special forces troops assisted the U.S. military in the war in Afghanistan. After the Taliban were defeated at the end of November, Blair tried to convince Bush to stay and build a stable and prosperous new nation.

But events were moving rapidly. Bush and his advisers were still convinced that Saddam Hussein's Iraq was a potential threat in the region, particularly if Saddam had weapons of mass destruction. Saddam had thrown out the UN weapons inspectors in 1998. He had had plenty of time to develop new weapons. British and U.S. intelligence reports indicated that, since 1998, Saddam had restarted his nuclear, biological, and chemical weapons programs. Sooner or later, some believed, he would be tempted to use them or, worse, sell them to a dangerous group such as al-Qaeda.

Many argued that Saddam had nothing to do with Islamic radicals, that he hated them and they him. Some also felt that Saddam had no weapons. It was true that he had used poison gas against Kurds in 1990, invaded his neighbors on two occasions, and murdered his own people. But years of UN sanctions (trade restrictions), weapons inspections, and the forced destruction of weapons had left the regime powerless.

But when Bush told Blair that after Afghanistan he would turn his attention to Iraq, Blair had agreed. He reasoned that sooner or later the Iraqi dictator's regime, which had ignored and defied UN sanctions for years, had to be dealt with.

THE PUSH FOR A DIPLOMATIC SOLUTION

Removing Saddam from power fit with Blair's political ideas. It was the right thing to do for several reasons. He felt that such an evil man and a killer of his own people should be replaced. The question was how to do it.

Speculation about a war with Iraq surfaced on television talk shows and newspaper articles. In Texas, in April 2002, Blair tried to persuade Bush to work through the United Nations. The UN could force Saddam to accept weapons inspectors, and if he refused, then a war would be legitimate. Blair and his aides thought that they had Bush's commitment to go to the UN.

In London several ministers in Blair's cabinet warned of dire consequences if the United States pushed for a unilateral war. Blair's attorney general, Lord Goldsmith, reportedly warned that an invasion of Iraq without a UN mandate (formal order) could be against international law. He also is said to have told Blair that even with UN support, Blair would have to prove to the UN that Iraq had intended to use weapons of mass destruction, posing an immediate threat.

Blair did not hear from Bush again until the end of July. The United States was moving steadily toward invading Iraq. Beyond the issue of whether Iraq had WMDs, the United States viewed Saddam as a potential threat to the region and the world.

In July Bush outlined a new U.S. foreign policy. He said that the United States would take preemptive military action (attack first) against perceived enemies of the United States.

This troubled Blair. He wrote Bush advising him that unless Bush went through the UN, Blair would face withering protests in his own government and in the streets of Great Britain. But disturbing reports were reaching him from his diplomats in Washington and at the UN in New York. The United States was ready to go it alone. Bush's senior advisers thought they had the justification needed to go to war with Iraq.

Finally, Bush went along with the wishes of Blair and U.S. secretary of state Colin Powell. Bush agreed to work through the UN. On September 12, George

Bush addressed the full membership of the United Nations in New York and the waiting world. He patiently listed all of Iraq's violations of UN resolutions. He called the UN "the world's most important multilateral body [organization of many nations]." And finally, he said, "We will work with the UN Security Council for the necessary resolutions."

TO WAR OR NOT TO WAR?

While Blair eloquently defended the case for toughness in dealing with Iraq, the Bush administration pushed ahead. Within one week of his speech to the UN, news reports and comments by the administration made it clear that the president was prepared to start the invasion of Iraq regardless of what the UN did. Many of Blair's European colleagues mistrusted George Bush.

Meanwhile, Blair had been pressuring his own intelligence service, MI6 (the British equivalent of the U.S. Central Intelligence Agency, or CIA), to provide him with proof that Saddam had WMDs. In September the Blair government released a fifty-page report with the evidence they had of Iraq's WMDs. One unverified report stated that Saddam had stocks of chemical and biological weapons that could be used within forty-five minutes. Some WMD experts objected that this couldn't be true, according to their estimates, but were told that the information came from the MI6 director. The press, Blair and his advisers, and Bush and his advisers repeated the information over and over again.

FORTY-FIVE MINUTES

In late May 2003, British Broadcasting Company (BBC) reporter Andrew Gilligan reported a sensational story that, if true, could have brought down the Blair government. Gilligan said on radio and television that Blair's claim in 2002 that Saddam had WMDs that could be used within forty-five minutes was untrue and Blair knew it. Gilligan had all but said that Blair had tricked the country into going to war.

Blair was furious. He denied the charge vehemently, and two parliamentary investigations found the charge against Blair to be untrue. The controversy continued until the name of a weapons inspector and scientist working for the British government, Dr. David Kelly, was put forward as the source of the leak to Gilligan. Kelly, a shy man, was thrust into the center of wild media attention. About the time that Blair was addressing the U.S. Congress on July 17, 2003, Kelly slashed his wrists and committed suicide.

The uproar was immense. Blair appointed a respected judge, Lord Hutton, to conduct an inquiry into Kelly's suicide. In the investigation, the prime minister testified, as did many others. When Lord Hutton finally released his report in late January 2004, he found no wrongdoing on the part of Blair or his government. The report was highly critical of Gilligan's reporting and of the BBC for allowing an inaccurate report to go on the air.

Blair had staked all his arguments on the existence of the weapons. All through October, the members of the UN Security Council argued over the wording of a UN resolution, the formal expression of the UN's will. Finally, on November 8, 2002, after bitter debate, Resolution 1441 passed unanimously. It offered Saddam a final opportunity to comply with all of the previous UN resolutions that he had ignored. He was to allow weapons inspectors complete access to all sites immediately.

If he did not comply, the French wanted a second resolution to decide the next step to be taken. The United States wanted an automatic trigger date, after which military action could immediately be taken. Blair's compromise won: if Saddam did not comply with the new resolution, the Security Council would meet again and decide what to do next.

But U.S. forces were already massing along the borders of Iraq, and Blair had given orders to mobilize twenty thousand British troops. These troops were there to encourage Saddam to comply with UN demands, but more and more, it seemed to many observers that the war was already planned and decided.

Blair could not convince French president Jacques Chirac and German chancellor Gerhardt Schroeder of George Bush's commitment to an international coalition against international terror. "Don't listen to the words. Watch what he does," Blair told them and other European leaders.

But by December, even many members of Blair's own party were convinced Bush wanted war no matter what. On December 8, Saddam delivered a twelve-thousand-page report on weapons in Iraq. It had no new information, so it seemed Saddam had defied the UN again. Both Blair and Bush decided that it was the end for the Iraqi leader.

But Blair had to make Bush keep his commitment to the international process, for the sake of the world and for Blair's political future. Dissent was growing in the Labour Party. Polls in Britain showed that the vast majority of the people opposed war in Iraq. Blair couldn't justify going to war to his party or his people without a second UN resolution. At the end of January 2003, Chirac and Schroeder jointly announced that "war is always an admission of defeat." They likely would not vote for another resolution. It looked as if Blair had failed to preserve European unity.

UN inspectors Hans Blix of Sweden and Mohamed El Baradei of the International Atomic Energy Agency reported to the UN in January 2003. Their inspection teams had not found any weapons of mass destruction, though large amounts of nerve gas seem to have disappeared, and Iraq was in violation of other inspection agreements.

The French and Germans argued against war since inspectors were in Iraq and the inspections were working. On February 5, Secretary of State Colin Powell, one of the few U.S. advisers to argue for

Mohamed El Baradei, right, and Hans Blix, left, speak at a press conference in 2002.

restraint, appeared at the UN. He presented the best evidence that the CIA could provide him that Iraq had WMDs. Nine days later, Blix again appeared before the UN and argued against Powell's evidence.

Blair went back and forth across the Atlantic, trying to make sure Bush would hold off until either Blix and the weapons inspectors could find stockpiles of chemicals or other WMDs, or the second resolution could be passed. Blix reported to the UN again in mid-February. He said that Saddam was cooperating and that inspections, while not finding anything, were being allowed to continue and expand into areas previously denied to them. They certainly had Saddam in a box. Still, the Bush administration pushed for war.

The next day, in cities worldwide, millions of people took to the streets protesting the obvious buildup to war—a war that was wanted only by the U.S. government and a loyal Tony Blair. More than one million people marched in protest in the cities of Britain—more than three-quarters of a million in London alone.

At a parliamentary test vote on February 26, Blair received approval for going to war because many of the Conservatives voted for it. But 121 Labour MPs voted against the war. Labour leaders warned Blair that if it came to an actual vote on the war, up to half of his own party, 200 members, were prepared to vote against him.

In mid-March it became clear that even if the United States agreed to seek another resolution approving the use of force, France and Germany would certainly vote against it. A resolution for force probably would not pass.

Blair was ill with a lingering cold, exhausted from his constant diplomatic efforts on behalf of George Bush, and depressed by his inability to make the U.S. president see the need for cooperation with Europe. All of his personal charm and his skills of argument and persuasion had failed him.

Then on March 10, French president Chirac declared that France would block the resolution for war "in all circumstances." Blair had promised Britain would not go to war unless another resolution authorized it. But if a veto such as Chirac's blocked the authorization, military action could still be taken under existing UN resolutions.

The world held its breath as all negotiations everywhere came to a halt. On March 16, Bush, Blair, and Spanish prime minister José Maria Aznar met in the Azore Islands in the Atlantic Ocean. The next day, President Bush announced he would not seek the second UN resolution and would go to war without UN approval. Blair was stunned, but he felt it was too late to do more than go along with the United States.

On March 18, before a call for a vote to authorize war, Tony Blair addressed the House of Commons. He called on the MPs to stand with him against the tyranny of Saddam's regime and the threats Saddam posed to his own people and the world. Blair spoke passionately. "This is not the time to falter," he said. "This is the time . . . to show that we will confront the tyrannies and dictatorships and terrorists who put our way of life at risk, to show at the moment of decision that we have the courage to do the right thing."

Three ministers resigned, and 139 Labour MPs voted against it, but the vote for war carried. There was no rejoicing. Twenty-four hours later, George Bush ordered an air strike on Baghdad, Iraq's capital, and Great Britain was at war.

Blair remains a powerful force in British politics, though his popularity with both his own party and the public has waned.

EPILOGUE

IN IRAQ AND AFTER

After British forces went into battle in Iraq, British public opinion shifted in support of its troops and the war. British forces occupied the southern port city of Basra within a week, and within three weeks, the U.S. Marines and Army were in Baghdad. On May 1, President Bush declared an end to major hostilities. Saddam's army had not used any chemical or biological agents. In fact, the Iraqi military had mostly just melted away.

But immediately after the declared end of the war, most of the country was plunged into chaos. Rioting and looting broke out, and water, telephone, and electric service was disrupted. The National Museum was robbed of many of its irreplaceable cultural objects. Despite the long run-up to the war, the British and U.S. coalition seemed unprepared for keeping the peace afterward.

Still, Tony Blair was seen as a man of courage and conviction, even by his sternest critics. On May 3, he celebrated his fiftieth birthday and was applauded as a statesman of the first rank.

Throughout the spring and summer of 2003, security in Baghdad and all over Iraq deteriorated. Various groups, angry at the occupation of Iraq, carried out assassinations and random murders. Terrorists used suicide car bombings against many civilian and military targets with deadly effect.

A prominent, moderate Muslim cleric (priest) was murdered. Then car bombers attacked the building housing the United Nations mission in Baghdad in mid-August, killing the head of the mission, Sergio Vieira de Mello, and twenty of his colleagues and staff.

In October hundreds of Iraqi worshippers were killed and wounded in the crowded streets of Karbala, Iraq, during a holy Muslim festival. Crime of all kinds—from robbery to rape and murder—increased in the streets of Baghdad. Law and order disappeared, and ordinary Iraqi citizens lived in danger.

Most experts think that these attacks were being carried out by radical Muslim groups, former political allies of Saddam, and members of al-Qaeda and other organizations, who see themselves as fighters in a struggle, a jihad, against the West. They wanted to make the country so chaotic that no one would be able to govern it.

AN UNEASY FUTURE

After receiving a Congressional Medal of Honor, Tony Blair addressed the U.S. Congress in July 2003. He said:

"Can we be sure that terrorism and weapons of mass destruction will join together? Let us say one thing. If we are wrong, we will have destroyed a threat that at least is responsible for inhuman carnage and suffering. That is something history will forgive. But if our critics are wrong, if we are right, as I believe with every fiber of instinct and conviction I have that we are, and we do not act, then we will have hesitated in the face of this menace, when we should have given leadership. That is something history will not forgive."

Following the fall of Baghdad, a CIA team of more than one thousand experts had found no stockpiles, not even one single WMD. After six months of searching, the director of the inspection team, David Kay, declared that everyone had been wrong. There were no WMDs. There probably weren't any at the time of the invasion, and Iraq's weapons programs had been shut down years earlier. The team also found no evidence of a nuclear program. It seems the earlier CIA information had been faulty.

U.S. special operations soldiers found Saddam in mid-December 2003 hiding in a hole in the ground not far from his hometown of Tikrit. Ironically, a year almost to the day that British and U.S. troops had entered Iraq, the situation in Iraq was worse, not better. Areas once thought to be peaceful and cooperative with coalition forces erupted in violence. Some of the heaviest fighting of the entire war occurred, not only in areas where Muslims loyal to Saddam lived, but in areas where Saddam was hated.

Terrorist violence in revenge for the Iraq invasion spread to Europe. In November 2003, Turkish suicide car bombers with links to al-Qaeda attacked two synagogues (Jewish places of worship) in Istanbul, Turkey. Two more suicide car bombers attacked a London-based bank and a British government office in Istanbul, killing twenty-seven.

In Madrid, Spain, on March 11, 2004, the eve of Spanish elections, ten bombs exploded on four commuter trains during rush hour killing 191 and wounding 1,800. The next day, a new Socialist government, opposed to the war, replaced the government of José Maria Aznar. Aznar, along with Blair, had been one of Bush's strongest allies in the Iraq invasion. The new Spanish Socialist president withdrew all of Spain's troops from Iraq.

In late April, more than fifty former and current British diplomats wrote an open letter to Blair. In it they bitterly criticized him for joining in Bush's war against Iraq. They felt that involvement in the war was making Great Britain many enemies and distracting efforts from the real war on terror—on al-Qaeda and organizations like it.

Blair, the statesman of deeply held moral beliefs, which he put into political practice, was having trouble convincing the country that he wasn't being duped by a U.S. president who was using him for his own ends. This was the dilemma Blair faced as spring turned to summer in 2004. In the June 2004 midterm elections, the Labour party lost 464 seats in Parliament, the worst performance ever recorded by a party in power. The vote against Labour was mainly because Blair had taken Great Britain into the Iraqi war. Blair's leadership faces opposition within the Labour Party itself, as Labour faces general elections in 2006. Only the passage of time and events in Iraq will determine how Blair will be viewed by future historians.

SOURCES

14 John Rentoul, *Tony Blair: Prime Minister*, (London: Time Warner Paperbacks, 2002), 9.
14 Kamal Ahmed, "Blair at 50: Childhood: Tony's Big Adventure," *Observer* (London), 27 April 2003, Review section.
15 Rentoul, 10.
16 Ibid., 11.
16 Ibid.
16 Ibid.
17 Ibid., 3.
17 Ibid.
18 Ibid., 5.
21 Kamal Ahmed, "Blair at 50: Teenage Years: 'He Could Always Talk His Way Out of Things,'" *Observer* (London), 27 April 2003, Review section.
22 Rentoul, 15.
23 Ibid., 16.
23 Ibid., 17.
24 Kamal Ahmed, "Blair at 50: Teenage Years: 'He Could Always Talk His Way Out of Things.'"
25 Ibid.
25 Rentoul, 21.
25 Ibid., 22.
26 Ibid., 28.
27 Ibid., 33.
28 Ibid., 43.
28 Ibid., 35.
28 Ibid.
29 Ibid., 41.
29 Ibid., 43.
29 Kamal Ahmed, "Blair at 50: Twenties: 'He Even Wanted to Rehearse,'" *Observer* (London), 27 April 2003, Review section.
29 Ibid.
30 Ibid.
30 Rentoul, 39.

31   Ibid., 48.
31   Ibid.
34   Ibid., 55.
34   Ibid., 63.
35   Ibid., 55–56.
38   Ibid., 85.
39   Ibid., 97.
39   Ibid.
41   Philip Stephens, *Tony Blair: The Making of a World Leader* (London: Viking Penguin, 2004), 39.
43   Rentoul, 122.
49   Stephens, 48.
51   John F. Kennedy, "Inaugural Address, January 20, 1961," *John F. Kennedy Library and Museum*, 2003, http://www.jfklibrary.org/j012061.htm (January 10, 2005).
51   Rentoul, 192.
52   Ibid., 200.
53   Ibid., 246.
53   Ibid.
57   Ibid., 314.
58   Ibid., 315.
59   Ibid., 332.
65   Stephens, 140.
67   Rentoul, 335.
67   Ibid., 336.
68   Ibid., 345.
69   Stephens, 147.
70   Ibid., 146.
71   Rentoul, 405.
76   Ibid., 515.
77   Ibid., 516.
77–78   Ibid., 521
79   Stephens, 163.
79   Rentoul, 528.
79   Ibid.
80   Stephens, 43.
80   Rentoul, 575.
85   Stephens, 187.
86   Ibid., 194.

87   Ibid., 197.
88   "Address to a Joint Session of Congress and the
        American People," White House, 2001,
        http://www.whitehouse.gov/
        news/releases/2001/09/20010920-8.html (January 10,
        2005).
89–90   Stephens, 201.
93   Bryan Burrough and others., "The Path to War," *Vanity
        Fair*, May 2004, Special Report section, 228.
95   Stephens, 222.
96   Ibid., 228.
98   Ibid., 235.
99   Ibid., 237.
102–103   Ibid., 244.

SELECTED BIBLIOGRAPHY

Blair, Tony. *New Britain: My Vision of a Young Country*. Boulder,
     CO: Westview Press, 2004.
Clarke, Richard A. *Against All Enemies: Inside America's War on
     Terror*. New York: Free Press, 2004.
Conford, Philip. *The Personal World: John Macmurray on Self and
     Society*. Edinburgh: Floris Books, 1997.
Rentoul, John. *Tony Blair: Prime Minister*. London: Time Warner
     Paperbacks, 2002.
Seldon, Anthony. *The Blair Effect*. Boston: Little, Brown and
     Company, 2001.
Stephens, Philip. *Tony Blair: The Making of a World Leader*.
     London: Viking Penguin, 2004.
Stothard, Peter. *Thirty Days: Tony Blair and the Test of History*.
     New York: HarperCollins, 2003.
Woodward, Bob. *Bush at War*. New York: Simon and Schuster, 2002.
———. *Plan of Attack*. New York: Simon and Schuster, 2004.

FURTHER READING
AND WEBSITES

BOOKS

Anderson, Dale. *Saddam Hussein*. Minneapolis: Lerner
Publications Company, 2004.

Hinman, Bonnie. *Tony Blair*. Philadelphia: Chelsea House
Publishers, 2003.

Katz, Sam. *Jihad: Islamic Fundamentalist Terrorism*. Minneapolis:
Lerner Publications Company, 2004.

Márquez, Herón. *George W. Bush*. Minneapolis: Lerner
Publications Company, 2002.

Naden, Corinne J., and Rose Blue. *Tony Blair*. San Diego: Lucent
Books, 2003.

Taus-Bolstad, Stacy. *Iraq in Pictures*. Minneapolis: Lerner
Publications Company, 2004.

Woolf, Alex. *Osama bin Laden*. Minneapolis: Lerner Publications
Company, 2004.

Zwier, Lawrence J., and Matthew S. Weltig. *The Persian Gulf and
Iraqi Wars*. Minneapolis: Lerner Publications Company, 2005.

WEBSITES

10 Downing Street
http://www.number-10.gov.uk/output/page4asp
The official website of the prime minister's office in Great Britain
includes a brief biography of Blair, along with news and
information about other government figures and activities.

"Tony Blair." *Wikipedia*
http://en.wikipedia.org/wiki/tony_blair
This site offers an extensive biography of Blair with links to
other people and events in his life.

INDEX

OTHER TITLES FROM LERNER AND A&E®:

Ariel Sharon
Arnold Schwarzenegger
Arthur Ashe
The Beatles
Benjamin Franklin
Bill Gates
Bruce Lee
Carl Sagan
Chief Crazy Horse
Christopher Reeve
Colin Powell
Daring Pirate Women
Edgar Allan Poe
Eleanor Roosevelt
Fidel Castro
George Lucas
George W. Bush
Gloria Estefan
Hillary Rodham Clinton
Jack London
Jacques Cousteau
Jane Austen
Jesse Owens
Jesse Ventura
Jimi Hendrix
John Glenn
Latin Sensations

Legends of Dracula
Legends of Santa Claus
Louisa May Alcott
Madeleine Albright
Malcolm X
Mark Twain
Maya Angelou
Mohandas Gandhi
Mother Teresa
Nelson Mandela
Oprah Winfrey
Osama bin Laden
Princess Diana
Queen Cleopatra
Queen Elizabeth I
Queen Latifah
Rosie O'Donnell
Saddam Hussein
Saint Joan of Arc
Thurgood Marshall
Tiger Woods
Vladimir Putin
William Shakespeare
Wilma Rudolph
Women in Space
Women of the Wild West
Yasser Arafat

ABOUT THE AUTHOR

Thomas M. Collins is a columnist and critic for the *Albuquerque Journal*. His writing and criticism have appeared in the *Los Angeles Times*, *Art in America*, *ArtNews*, *American Ceramics*, and numerous other publications.

PHOTO ACKNOWLEDGMENTS

Photographs used with the permission of: Office of the Prime Minister, p. 2; © Graeme Robertson/Getty Images, p. 6; © Manuel Blondeau/CORBIS, p. 8; Sipa/Rex Features USA, p. 10; © CORBIS SYGMA, pp. 12, 18; © Fox Photos/Getty Images, p. 15; Alan Forbes, Edinburgh, Scotland, p. 20; SWS/Rex Features USA, p. 27; © PA/EMPICS, p. 32; © Hulton Archive/Getty Images, p. 35; Bucks Free Press, p. 37; Newsquest Northeast LTD, p. 40; Guardian Newspapers Limited, 1988, p. 42; Philip Dunn/Rex Features USA, p. 46; Guardian Newspapers Limited, 1993, p. 48; Weir Stewart/CORBIS SYGMA, p. 54; Rooke/Jorgensen/Rex Features USA, p. 56; AP/Wide World Photos, p. 59; © Hulton-Deutsch Collection/CORBIS, p. 64; © Andrew Murray/CORBIS, p. 66; © Cynthia Johnson/Liaison/Getty Images, p. 70 (left); © James Leynse/CORBIS, p. 70 (right); © Richard Open/Camera Press/Retna Ltd., USA, p. 72; © Grazia Neri/R. Arcari/CORBIS SYGMA, p. 78; © ROTA/All Action/Retna Ltd., USA, p. 81; © Reuters/CORBIS, p. 84; © Baci/CORBIS, p. 89; © Paul Assaker/CORBIS, p. 97; © Camera Press/ROTA/Retna Ltd., USA, p. 100.
Cover photos (hard and soft cover): front, © Reuters/CORBIS; back, © Neil Libbert.

WEBSITES